Mac

By George Forbes

Lang**Syne**

PUBLISHING

WRITING *to* REMEMBER

Lang**Syne**

PUBLISHING

WRITING *to* REMEMBER

79 Main Street, Newtongrange,
Midlothian EH22 4NA
Tel: 0131 344 0414   Fax: 0845 075 6085
E-mail: info@lang-syne.co.uk
www.langsyneshop.co.uk

Design by Dorothy Meikle
Printed by Ricoh Print Scotland
© Lang Syne Publishers Ltd 2014

ISBN 978-1-85217-093-6

MacLennan

SEPT NAMES:

Gilfillian
Lennan
Lennon
Leonard
Loban
Lobban
Logan
Lyndon
MacAlonan
MacClennen
MacLenden
MacLennan
MacLennon
MacLyndon
McLennan

MacLennan

MOTTO:
While I breathe I hope.

CREST:
A piper.

TERRITORY:
Wester Ross and Cromarty.

Chapter one:

The origins of the clan system

by Rennie McOwan

The original Scottish clans of the Highlands and the great families of the Lowlands and Borders were gatherings of families, relatives, allies and neighbours for mutual protection against rivals or invaders.

Scotland experienced invasion from the Vikings, the Romans and English armies from the south. The Norman invasion of what is now England also had an influence on land-holding in Scotland. Some of these invaders stayed on and in time became 'Scottish'.

The word clan derives from the Gaelic language term 'clann', meaning children, and it was first used many centuries ago as communities were formed around tribal lands in glens and mountain fastnesses.

The format of clans changed over the centuries, but at its best the chief and his family held the land on behalf of all, like trustees, and the ordinary clansmen and women believed they had a blood relationship with the founder of their clan.

There were two way duties and obligations. An inadequate chief could be deposed and replaced by someone of greater ability.

Clan people had an immense pride in race. Their relationship with the chief was like adult children to a father and they had a real dignity.

The concept of clanship is very old and a more feudal notion of authority gradually crept in.

Pictland, for instance, was divided into seven principalities ruled by feudal leaders who were the strongest and most charismatic leaders of their particular groups.

By the sixth century the 'British' kingdoms of Strathclyde, Lothian and Celtic Dalriada (Argyll) had emerged and Scotland, as one nation, began to take shape in the time of King Kenneth MacAlpin.

Some chiefs claimed descent from

ancient kings which may not have been accurate in every case.

By the twelfth and thirteenth centuries the clans and families were more strongly brought under the central control of Scottish monarchs.

Lands were awarded and administered more and more under royal favour, yet the power of the area clan chiefs was still very great.

The long wars to ensure Scotland's independence against the expansionist ideas of English monarchs extended the influence of some clans and reduced the lands of others.

Those who supported Scotland's greatest king, Robert the Bruce, were awarded the territories of the families who had opposed his claim to the Scottish throne.

In the Scottish Borders country – the notorious Debatable Lands – the great families built up a ferocious reputation for providing warlike men accustomed to raiding into England and occasionally fighting one another.

Chiefs had the power to dispense justice and to confiscate lands and clan warfare produced a society where martial virtues – courage, hardiness, tenacity – were greatly admired.

Gradually the relationship between the clans and the Crown became strained as Scottish monarchs became more orientated to life in the Lowlands and, on occasion, towards England.

The Highland clans spoke a different language, Gaelic, whereas the language of Lowland Scotland and the court was Scots and in more modern times, English.

Highlanders dressed differently, had different customs, and their wild mountain land sometimes seemed almost foreign to people living in the Lowlands.

It must be emphasised that Gaelic culture was very rich and story-telling, poetry, piping, the clarsach (harp) and other music all flourished and were greatly respected.

Highland culture was different from other parts of Scotland but it was not inferior or less sophisticated.

Central Government, whether in London or Edinburgh, sometimes saw the Gaelic clans as

"The spirit of the clan means much to thousands of people"

a challenge to their authority and some sent expeditions into the Highlands and west to crush the power of the Lords of the Isles.

Nevertheless, when the eighteenth century Jacobite Risings came along the cause of the Stuarts was mainly supported by Highland clans.

The word Jacobite comes from the Latin for James – Jacobus. The Jacobites wanted to restore the exiled Stuarts to the throne of Britain.

The monarchies of Scotland and England became one in 1603 when King James VI of Scotland (1st of England) gained the English throne after Queen Elizabeth died.

The Union of Parliaments of Scotland and England, the Treaty of Union, took place in 1707.

Some Highland clans, of course, and Lowland families opposed the Jacobites and supported the incoming Hanoverians.

After the Jacobite cause finally went down at Culloden in 1746 a kind of ethnic cleansing took place. The power of the chiefs was curtailed. Tartan and the pipes were banned in law.

Many emigrated, some because they

wanted to, some because they were evicted by force. In addition, many Highlanders left for the cities of the south to seek work.

Many of the clan lands became home to sheep and deer shooting estates.

But the warlike traditions of the clans and the great Lowland and Border families lived on, with their descendants fighting bravely for freedom in two world wars.

Remember the men from whence you came, says the Gaelic proverb, and to that could be added the role of many heroic women.

The spirit of the clan, of having roots, whether Highland or Lowland, means much to thousands of people.

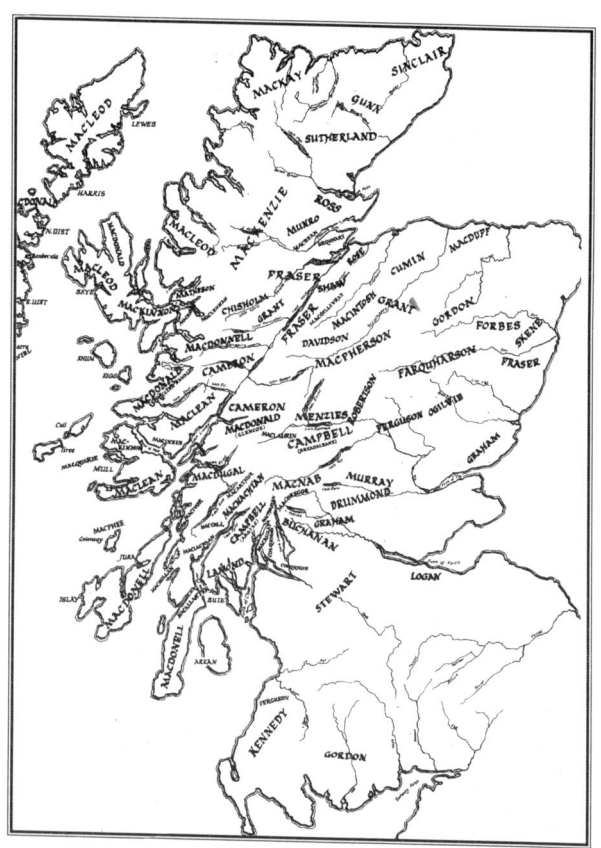

A map of the clans' homelands

Chapter two:

Monks and massacres

In Gaelic the name MacLennan is rendered as 'MacGille Finnan' which means 'the son of the follower of St. Finnan.'

Who exactly this refers to has now been lost in the distant past; and the history of this clan is made even more complex by the fact that until as late as 1976 there had not been a recognised chief for more than 300 years.

Part of the reason for the lack of a detailed historical record stems from the sheer necessity of survival for a small group on the fringes of Highland society who had to ally themselves with more powerful neighbours simply to retain any form of independence in the feudal war zone of medieval clan society.

Thus the story of the MacLennans is inextricably linked with those of their neighbouring comrades like the Macraes and the MacKenzies.

The first known MacLennans initially

settled around Kintail and were related to the Logans who also held lands in Easter Ross, though the latter were to become more prominent in the Central Lowlands as Barons of Restalrig near the Port of Leith.

In fact some historians claim that the MacLennans were actually just a branch of the Logans and that their name was not properly adopted in its present form until the fifteenth century.

According to this version of the family's origins, Gillegorm Logan led his clansmen towards Inverness to continue a typical Highland blood feud against the Frasers.

Gillegorm was ambushed at Kessock, a hamlet two miles north west of Inverness, and he and most of his followers were brutally slain. In those days taking prisoners was seen as a sign of weakness.

However, the Frasers did capture alive Logan's pregnant wife, intending either to kill the child when born or perhaps raise him as a fosterling, a common Highland method of gaining influence over a rival clan.

The son was eventually allowed to be born but was so deformed that he was placed with the monks at Beauly where he quietly studied, entering the church when he reached maturity.

However, he blithely disregarded the decree of Pope Innocent III enforcing celibacy on the priesthood, preferring to follow the older, more relaxed Celtic practices.

He could not have been that ugly in his adulthood for he married and had several sturdy sons.

He took the name 'Gille Finnan' and his family honoured his memory by adopting this new name.

Regardless of the authenticity of this tradition, the heraldry of the chief does proclaim the link between the Logans and the MacLennans.

Each bears the heart and passion nails which refer to the pilgrimage of Sir Robert and Walter Logan who accompanied the embalmed heart of Robert the Bruce, kept in a silver casket, which was meant to end up in the Holy Land.

But, along with their leader, Sir James

Douglas (popularly known as 'the Black Douglas'), they were diverted in Spain by a crusade involving the local Christian knights against the 'heathen' Moors.

Douglas was killed at the battle of Teba and the knights returned home to Scotland where Bruce's heart was eventually buried in the grounds of Melrose Abbey in the Borders.

The MacLennan shield also alludes to their close connection with the Mackenzies whose banner was the 'caber-feidh', so called because of the deer's head in the centre.

Along with the Macraes, the MacLennans remained for centuries the staunchest supporters of the Mackenzies; and at one time were custodians of their mighty fortress at Eilean Donan on its rocky islet at the entrance to Loch Duich in scenic Wester Ross.

It was in the service of the Mackenzie chieftain that the MacLennans came to prominence.

The Marquis of Montrose had rallied many Highland clans to the Royalist banner in 1645: but he was equally opposed by many others, including the Covenanting Earl of Seaforth, at that time chief of the Mackenzies.

The men of Kintail, led by the MacLennan chief, Ruaridh, a red-bearded giant who towered well over six feet, followed Lord Seaforth's standard.

The Covenanters fought Montrose at Auldearn, two miles south east of Nairn, on May 9th, 1645.

Montrose was heavily outnumbered but used his tactical genius to deceive his enemies, massing his banners to confuse them with regards to the strength and positioning of his forces.

His ruse succeeded and the Covenanters massed for a full frontal assault which gave Montrose the opportunity to outflank them and turn the battle in his favour.

The MacLennans had been sent an order to withdraw but in the chaos of the battle it was never delivered; so Ruaridh and his clansmen bravely if vainly fought on to the last, defending their banner. They were eventually decimated by the Gordon cavalry.

*Clan warfare produced a society where
courage and tenacity were greatly admired*

Chapter three:

Highlands vs islands

The MacLennans also were allies with the Mackenzies in their seemingly interminable, centuries-old feuding with the Lords of the Isles.

This was a Highland versus Island dispute over territory and power, resulting in numerous battles and atrocities being committed by both sides along Scotland's rugged north-western coastline.

On one occasion, in the fifteenth century, the MacDonalds of the Isles with an army of more than three thousand rampaging clansmen invaded the mainland fiefdoms of the MacLennans, MacKenzies and Macraes.

They went on to attack Inverness, plundered much of the north-east then retraced their steps back through Strathconnon, putting many who crossed their path to the sword.

They arrived at last at a church which they

set on fire, even though terrified old men, women and children were cowering inside, having taken shelter there in the mistaken belief that they would be safe. They were all brutally burned to death.

This dreadful massacre proved the final straw for the Highland confederation of clans who, the following day, though outnumbered, clashed with the invading MacDonalds in a bloody encounter that became known as the Battle of the Parks.

The Highlanders, numbering only around 600, attacked first and then immediately retreated in a favourite ploy aimed at entrapment.

The scheme worked and the MacDonalds heedlessly chased after them and within minutes literally became bogged down in a marshy wasteland.

At this point MacLennan archers, hidden among bushes in the flanks, fired off a withering fusillade and the arrows sliced devastatingly into the ranks of the islanders who collapsed mortally wounded in droves.

Their allies the Mackenzies then turned in

their seemingly headlong retreat and stormed back into the fray.

There was brutal hand-to-hand fighting as scarlet claymores sliced through the air and the normally tranquil countryside echoed with the screams of the dying and the angry shouts of the victors.

As the sun began to set on the grim scene, the MacDonalds took to their heels back to their fastnesses in the west.

This battle weakened the power of the island raiders but strengthened that of the mainland clans, including the MacLennans, who vowed loyalty to the Crown.

The King and his Highland allies had similar interests - the destruction of the MacDonalds' brutal rule in the Western Isles.

This was accomplished in 1493 when the Lordship of the Isles was forfeited; and thereafter the MacLennans and their allies were adept at intervening in island disputes and seizing land weakened by internal dissension or outside pressure.

Thus property owned by the MacLeods

on Lewis was seized, as were lucrative estates on other islands.

The MacLennans were active in the Jacobite Rebellions supporting the Stuart cause, most notably during the summer of 1719 when a large Spanish fleet set sail for Scotland but was scattered and wrecked during a severe freak storm among the savage rocks of the west coast.

A group of several hundred MacLennans had mustered to meet up with these foreign troops; so when two of the ships actually managed to get through with the MacKenzie chief, the Earl of Seaforth, on board the first, the MacLennans were there to form a welcoming party when they landed at Eilean Donan Castle.

Meanwhile, a force of 1,000 infantry was on the march from Inverness to intercept the ill-fated uprising.

The Jacobites took up a strong position at the head of Loch Duich, eight miles south-east of Kyle of Lochalsh.

The rocks, high ground and entrench-ments suited the Highlanders whereas the advancing redcoats were apprehensive and cautious, being in the midst of hostile territory.

Both sides were evenly matched but the morale of the rebels seems to have been a lot lower than their opponents.

The redcoats had four light bronze mortars which should not have been enough to sway the day but the Spaniards, like the government troops, were also trapped on foreign soil and their hearts did not seem to be in the fight.

The redcoats' commander, General Wightman, a veteran of the earlier Jacobite defeat at Sheriffmuir in 1715, fought an impeccable action, though he was helped by the lack of determination on the part of his opponents.

After ordering a charge uphill against his foes, he lost no more than 21 men killed and 121 wounded.

The Jacobite losses were similar but many of them decided discretion was the better part of valour and took to their heels, shamefully leaving their Spanish allies to their fate.

Bewildered and disheartened, the Spanish

eventually flung down their muskets in disgust.

As Wightman drily remarked, "Every-one else took the road he liked best."

Seaforth, badly wounded, had to flee to the Continent with a price on his head.

Meanwhile, Eilean Donan was blown up and demolished by the victorious government forces, determined to destroy the rebels' stronghold once and for all.

This most romantic of Scottish castles was not fully restored until the twentieth century.

The Spanish captives were moved under armed escort to Inverness and then to Edinburgh. Their condition aroused much sympathy; and, finally, after just a few months in captivity, they were allowed to sail home again.

Their only memorial is a corrie far up the hill in the Pass of Strachell that overlooked the fight in Glen Shiel which is now known as the 'Bealach na Spainnteach' or 'the Spaniards' Pass'.

Following this dismal rebellion, the lands of the MacLennans were garrisoned by government troops to keep the restless natives under control.

It was to be another 26 years before the Stuarts made another doomed attempt to regain the British throne.

The MacLennan clansmen were among those who rallied to Bonnie Prince Charlie's flag at Glenfinnan in 1745 and accompanied him on his triumphal march into Edinburgh.

They were also in the leading ranks of the charging Highlanders who disturbed the morning slumbers of General Cope's government troops when they came rampaging out of the dawn mists at Prestonpans.

The MacLennans went on all the way south to Derby and remained loyal in the ranks when the Young Pretender's gradually disintegrating force fought their opponents to an indecisive halt at Falkirk.

There were also MacLennans mown down by 'Butcher' Cumberland's artillery on Drummossie Moor, better known to posterity as the battle of Culloden, which proved yet another defeat for the Jacobite cause, this time a final one.

The Battle of Culloden

Chapter four:

The champion pipers

Eleven MacLennans are recorded as having been taken prisoner after the final defeat of the Jacobites at Culloden, though their eventual fate is not known.

Probably, as mere foot soldiers in the defeated army, they would have been exiled as slaves to the colonies, if they did not die first in the filthy, disease-ridden prison hulks moored in the muddy Thames off Tilbury.

Following this devastating rout, the clan system was ripped apart in the wild north and, like other Highland families, many MacLennans, forced out of their burning cottages, had to emigrate abroad or starve to death.

Their presence is detectable in the naming of the MacLennan Mountains of New Zealand and in MacLennan County, Texas.

Ronald MacLennan of MacLennan was duly recognised by the Lord Lyon, King of Arms, as chief of this name under the process of selection known as the 'ad hoc derbhfine'.

He was not a bloodline chief, although he was a member of the only MacLennan family to have matriculated arms since 1672.

He carried out a great deal of research into his clan's history and published this in 1978, tracing the clan's origins to the ancient royal Celtic families of Ireland and Scotland through Aengus Macgillafinan, Lord of Loch-erne around 1230.

The family also developed a great tradition as pipers.

MacLennans were town pipers in Inverness in the early sixteenth century, played at the battle of Waterloo and have regularly won modern competitions.

This is suitably commemorated by a piper blowing merrily away on the clan crest.

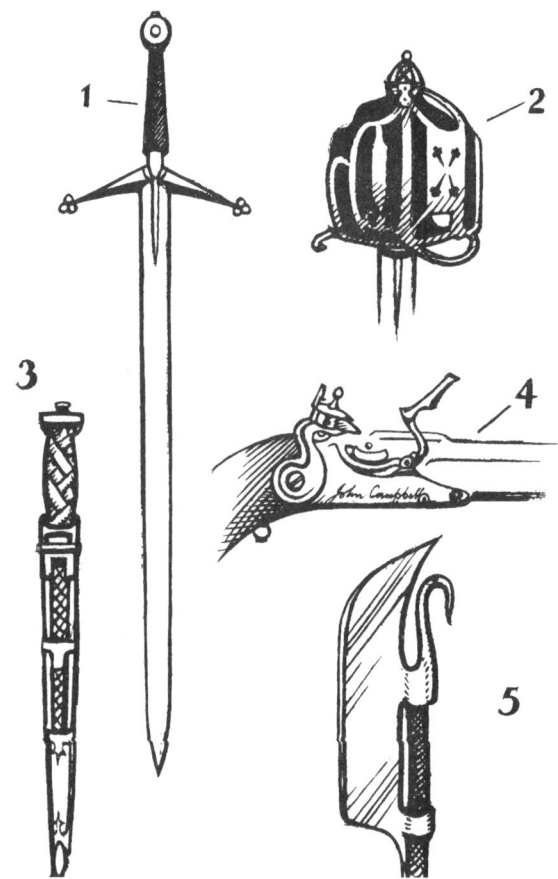

Highland weapons

1) The claymore or two-handed sword
   (fifteenth or early sixteenth century)

2) Basket hilt of broadsword
   made in Stirling, 1716

3) Highland dirk
   (eighteenth century)

4) Steel pistol *(detail)* made in Doune

5) Head of Lochaber Axe as carried
   in the '45 and earlier